OF SMILES AND TEARS

Very Best Wishes
To Bill. Bob S.
Robert J. Singleton 12/17/11

Of Smiles and Tears

Robert J. Singleton

Copyright © 2011 by Robert J. Singleton.

Library of Congress Control Number:		2011912458
ISBN:	Hardcover	978-1-4628-4789-1
	Softcover	978-1-4628-4788-4
	Ebook	978-1-4628-4790-7

All rights reserved. No part of this book may be reproduced or transmitted in any form or by any means, electronic or mechanical, including photocopying, recording, or by any information storage and retrieval system, without permission in writing from the copyright owner.

This book was printed in the United States of America.

To order additional copies of this book, contact:
Xlibris Corporation
1-888-795-4274
www.Xlibris.com
Orders@Xlibris.com

CONTENTS

Of Smiles and Tears 9
Your Hands 10
Your Beauty 11
When I'm Away 12
The Cuckoo Clock 13
What True Love Is 14
The Clock 15
Today At The Lake 16
The Painting... 17
Thoughts On Fall... 18
The Candle 19
Things I Should Have Said 20
The Friend... 21
My Heart and Hands 22
Loving You.. 23
The Setting Sun 24
The Morning Sun 25
Stormy Nights 26
The Forest Path 27
If I Could 28
Seasons of Love 29
Dreaming 30
Quiet Times 31
What is a Rose?... 32
Reaching Out Your Hand 33
Before You Love 34
The Ways I Love You.. 35
A Rose... 36
A Prisoner 37

On Aging	38
Your Golden Years	39
Morning Coffee	40
Waiting For You	41
Looking At You	42
Consolation	43
Forest Across The Lake	44
A Lasting Love	45
Dust On The Bible	46
Your Smile	47
Easter Lilies	48
A Smile and A Tear	49
Coming Home	50
A Valentine	51
Changes	52
Because I Care	53
Autumn Walk In The Woods	54
Death	55
Winter's Warmth	56
Discovering Peace	57
The Park Gate	58
Hidden Tears	59
Daises	60
In Search of Riches	61
What is Love	62
Journey's End	63
Autumn	64
My Heart	65
A Walk in the Woods	66
I Can't Love You Any More!	67
Remembering	68
Roses	69
When We Are Apart	70
Spring	71
My Love For You	72
The Sentinel	73

Walking With You	74
Broken Glass	75
You're Feeling Sorry	76
Silently Sleeping	77
Soaring	78
Thanking You	79
On Being Sorry	80
This Special Rose	81
Treasure Every Friend	82
Before I Say Goodnight	83
Believing In Love	84
Honesty	85
On Autumn	86
Blossoming Flowers	87
Missing You	88
Chances at Love	89
Judge Tenderly of Me	90
To Thank You	91
On Loving You	92
Silent Tears	93
The Old Lighthouse	94
Walking In The Rain	95
The Quiet Lake	96
Rose Thorns	97
The Sea	98
The Tip of Your Finger	99
Prince of Fools	100
Visions of You	101
Winter Wayfarer	102
Butterflies	103
To Hope for Love	104
Jealousy	105
To Dream	106
Another Tear	107
A Fallen Angel	108
Christmas Without You	110

To Be Free 111
Ageless Love 112
To One Who Is Missed 113
Before I Knew Your Name 114
Upon Leaving 115
Christmas Gifts 116
Liking You 117
I Heard the Bluebird Singing 118
A Letter of Doubt 119
In Love Again 120
Philosophy for Winter 121
It Rained Today 122
On Winter 123
Just Because 124
My Falling Tears 125
No Angel on the Christmas Tree 126
Lady on the Street 127
On Having Faith 128
The Old Man Alone at Christmas 129
The Green Sequined Gown 130
This Band of Gold 131
This Heart Full of Love 132
To Ask Forgiveness 133
Walk with Me 134
What I See 135
4th Of July 136
These Arms 137
Forever Springtime 138
A Cloud 139
Another Autumn 140
If You Could Love Me 141
Of Smiles and Tears 142

Of Smiles and Tears . . .

There is a land within men's minds
　　where few are free to go
To roam among the broken dreams
　　of seeds that thoughts have sown.
Who shall name this virgin land,
　　this land of smiles and tears?
It has no name for when men die
　　their thoughts like ashes disappear.

Your Hands

I remember the first time we met, and you took my hand in yours and said hello. Then you let me hold your hand as we walked beside a lake, or down a forest path. And you had this way of pressing on my hand whenever I said something to make you laugh. When I held your hand in the movie theatre, it was you who pulled away and placed my arm around you. And as I squeezed you in my arms you let me kiss you on the cheek. And you took my other hand in yours and gently pressed against it. to let me know everything was alright. As time went by, there were those moments when we danced, and you pressed my hand in yours to show me you cared. As I look back on it now I realize it was your hands that led the way to your heart. Now as I rest snugly in your heart, I still find pleasure in reaching across a dinner table and holding your hands. And when I do this, I see the sparkle in your eyes. I feel like the same boy who you once let hold your hands. I know you often frown when you look at your hands. The years have taken their toll on both of us. But I want you to know I will never tire of holding your hands. Because I know as I hold your hands, you are holding my heart. A heart that will always love you for holding my hands.

Your Beauty

There is beauty everywhere,
in everything we hear and see.
The moon, the stars, a sunny day,
a stately weeping willow tree.
But all the sights we marvel at,
all the songs the bluebirds sing,
Grow dim each time I think of you,
and all the joy your smile brings.
You make rainbows everyday
and storm clouds disappear,
And in my heart there's happiness,
because it's glad that you are there.
Nature paints a masterpiece,
I'll grant this may be true,
But I see beauty beyond compare,
each time I look at you.

When I'm Away

It's not unusual for you to wonder if I think about you when I'm away from you. Let me ease your mind in this way. Whenever I meet a stranger and they ask me why I am always smiling and seem so happy, I always tell them it is because I have such a beautiful lady waiting for me at home. When someone compliments me on the clothes I am wearing, I always tell them you pick out the clothes I wear. When I am alone, I find myself whistling a happy tune, because I am thinking about you. and wondering what you are doing. I always walk a little faster as I head home knowing you will be waiting for me with a hug and a kiss. I try to imagine what pleasant odors I will find coming from the kitchen., a meal fit for a king, lovingly prepared by you. The next time you wonder if I think about you when I'm away from you, just know that I can think of nothing else. Your love has filled my heart. There is no room for anything else in my heart. Thoughts of you have filled my mind to overflowing.

The Cuckoo Clock

Tick, tock, tick tock, endless syncopation.
Tick tock, tick tock, and quiet anticipation.
Old cuckoo clock, you're rightly named,
You cuckoo each new hour changed.
And when the minutes pass too slow,
You cuckoo early to let us know.
But what of cuckoos with no mean,
Why cuckoo you for causes unseen?
To fix you would only take away,
The thrill of unexpected cuckooed days.
Cuckoo on my troubled friend,
Your cuckoos reassure us we are only men.

What True Love Is

There are times and places we store in our mind because they are special to us. And quite often we use the word love to describe them. I love being in the mountains, feeling the clear fresh air blowing the aroma of sweet smelling pines and being overwhelmed by their vastness. I love the sound of a fast running brook, seeing the trout rising to the surface, feasting on the Mayflies. I love seeing the animals in the forest, trusting and at the same time being timid, always ready to run from this strange intruder into their domain. I love lying in a field of clover and looking up at the clouds drifting by. Like so many other people, I overused the word love. I took for granted a feeling I really did not understand. Without my realizing what was happening;, you taught me what love is. When I am in the mountains, the cool fresh air, the sweet smelling pines, remind me of you. I hear your laugh in the fast running brook, I see your face, your smile, in every passing cloud. Love could be just a word I use; unless you were a part of it. Being with you and holding you in my arms gives new meaning to all the things I thought I loved. Love is caring for someone and knowing they care for you. All the world is beautiful when you let someone into your heart and they show you what true love is.

The Clock

Tick tock, tick tock,
There is love within me beating,
Like the rhythm of a clock,
And your name I keep repeating.
Tick tock, tick tock.
Many reasons why I love you,
You have given me new life.
And I hope you love me also,
Someday soon to be my wife.
Tick tock, tick tock.
I have always wanted children,
Longed for warmth that is called home.
In your arms I'll stay forever,
Nevermore I care to roam.
Tick tock, tick tock.
Gentle tears from you keep falling,
Such joy is given from above.
He will truly bless our marriage,
Do not be afraid to love.
Tick tock, tick tock.

Today At The Lake

Something unexpected happened today as I walked along the lake. A tear fell from my eye. It has been a long while since I let a thing like that happen to me. And then I realized it was because of all of you on the Internet. It is our friendship towards each other that makes a person feel human again and susceptible to releasing our inner feelings. Then as I walked along, more tears fell. But they were not tears for myself, they were tears for all of you and the losses you have suffered. As I walked along in the warm sunlight, I wished that this same sun would warm all of you and that the calm serenity I saw looking upon the lake would calm your spirits and give you peace of mind. The sun will rise again tomorrow, and it's warmth will lighten our spirits, as it did for me; today at the lake.

The Painting

If I could paint a picture,
Bringing all life's beauty into view,
Darling it would be a masterpiece,
The picture I would paint of you.
For brightness I would try to paint,
The sunlight glowing in your hair,
And yes I'd paint your loving smile,
For all to see and share.
But the warmth and love that's in your heart,
I'd never let be shown,
That's one painting I would keep,
And treasure for my own.

Thoughts On Fall

Fall has become my favorite time of the year. Walking through the cool forest, marveling at the many colors the leaves change into. Once I dreaded walking through the forest in the Fall. Each falling leaf was accompanied by a tear falling from my eyes. Past memories of lovers long gone away, can do that to you if you let it. Then one day I felt the warm rays of the sun shining through the leafless trees. Rays that warm you the way friends warm your heart. Looking above the trees the white, billowing clouds reminded me of the smiles of people I see each day. Happiness can be found walking through a forest in the Fall. Rather than being the end of another year, the Fall is a continuation of the time we have to enjoy our lives and to take a moment to thank Him, for letting us enjoy His Fall Season and all the beauty that abounds at this time of the year.

The Candle

Keep a candle burning,
In the window of your heart.
From strange roads I will be turning,
And you'll guide me in the dark.
Keep a candle burning,
Lest I lose my way.
In cold my heart is yearning,
For the warmth your love conveys.
Keep a candle burning,
For there's trouble in the night.
To your heart I'll be returning,
For the love I found tonight.

Things I Should Have Said

When we walked together hand in hand, I should have told you, you were also holding onto my heart. And now I'm left alone, with only half a heart. When we held each other in our arms, my voiceless mind kept shouting "Never let her go!" Now I "The Prince of Fools" am standing here all alone. Hiding my face so that my loneliness will never show. If we should ever meet again and you allow your hand to merge with mine, you will not leave with only half my heart, you will have it all. And the voice you hear will speak of the love that's in my heart and on my mind.

The Friend

I am a friend of Michael's,
And he's told me of your plans
How you and he were to marry,
And how he's such a lucky man.
You're as pretty as your picture,
He's shown it off so much.
The fellows used to kid him so,
At times he'd even blush.
Your picture's worn and tattered now,
It aged in such a short time
And men grow weary just as fast,
From the road of life they climb.
No, he didn't come home with me,
You see, that's why I'm here.
Michael won't be coming home,
He died saving my life, my dear.

My Heart and Hands

When I was young, my heart and eyes were jealous of my hands. Because those hands could touch you and feel your softness and your warmth. And then, when I was not yours to touch, my eyes became the most important of my senses. Because those eyes could see what my hands longed to touch. And now, as the years pass by, it is my eyes and hands that are jealous of my heart. Because my heart has stored away what my eyes have seen, and my hands have touched. Where my eyes and hands are empty, longing for what once was; my heart is happy. Because in my heart my thoughts and love for you remains constant. If something happens to me in the near future. And my eyes are closed forever. My hands lay still. Do not wonder if I finally stopped loving you. My love for you will live forever in my spirit. And in the night winds, you will hear me forever calling your name.

Loving You

Time has dimmed the sunlight in my face,
And turned a youthful head a silver gray.
While in my heart the years have not erased,
Your beauty that I saw on that first day.
In my heart your beauty does not fade,
My love holds back the minute hands of time.
You walk through life beneath my loving shade,
That guards you from the sunlight's harshest time.
But I grow old with every passing day,
Each Winters cut a furrow in my brow.
'Till I fear you'll look at me and say,
"Who is this stranger who calls upon me now?"
If I must walk alone life's ending path,
I'll not look back on all that might have been.
Because my heart will think of you and laugh,
For loving you has been my only sin.

The Setting Sun

Just as the setting sun shines its last gleaming rays upon the sleepy forest, the memory of your smile brightens my heart as this day is finally coming to an end. There are no sounds deep down in the darkened forest floor. The birds must already have found a safe nesting place and they too make no sound. Amidst all this peaceful quiet, I hear your laugh and I look for you deep into the fading light escaping the forest floor, The sound of your laugh, the brightness of your smile will keep me warm and contented as the night approaches. If you were near, you would hear me thank you for the friendship you have offered me. A friendship I treasure because it is so freely given. And if you were near I would hold you in my arms as we watched the sunset together. Not being sad because of the coming of night but only knowing the happiness that comes from sharing a quiet moment like this together. And I would thank you, over and over again, for just being you. And for being here with me, if only in my mind as I watched the setting sun.

The Morning Sun

Each morning the sun shines through the bedroom window and lands upon my face on my side of the bed. I always wondered why you insisted I take this side of the bed but now as I rise up to go make the coffee, I understand why. As I look back at you laying in the bed I think I see the hint of a smile on your face although you appear to still be sleeping. If you knew how much I love you and enjoy doing things for you, you wouldn't feel so smug about putting one over on me. Bringing you your coffee in bed is only one of the ways I can thank you for just being you and for loving me. Going about our daily lives my thoughts of you are stored in the back of my heart. Getting through the day requires all my attention but when I come home and you are waiting there for me, all the day's frustrations melt away. Having your arms around me, and feeling you hold me tight makes me feel warm and content and I am thankful for having the love of such a beautiful lady. Each moment I spend with you are special moments. But the moment I treasure most. is being able to bring you your morning coffee after being wakened up by the morning sun.

Stormy Nights

I walk alone on stormy nights,
And drink the bitter vetch of rain.
The winds of me take fresh delights,
As they blow across the plains.
The trees with branches bending low,
Are strangers in the lightning's glow.
Howling winds shrill voices saying,
"Your love beneath cold ground is laying."
Many rains have bathed my face,
Of hopes new loves would take her place.
And I delight in nights so drear,
Only the storm can see my tears.

The Forest Path

With the dawning of each new day I walk alone upon the forest path. And each time I think how nice it would be to have you walking here beside me. I also know how vulnerable I would be if you were here. Walking alone my heart can drink in the beauty of all that I see in the forest. A beauty I never noticed until you came into my life. And shared your love with me. If you were walking beside me, the silence of the still sleeping forest would be broken. Broken by my voice, telling you of my love and how happy you have made me. The mist rising from the forest floor would help disguise the mist that fills my eyes each time I look at you. The animals that run and hide from me would never run away if you were with me. Animals can sense the gentleness that lies within each person passing by on the forest path and I am too jealous to share your gentleness with even the lowly forest animals. High up in the trees the birds singing to greet the new day would be drowned out by the singing coming from my heart. You would hear the songs of love that I keep hidden deep inside me and you would know that I am trapped forever by my love for you. I am only fooling myself by not asking you to walk with me along the forest path. In my mind I can think I don't need your company but in my heart there is a tender pain. A longing that will never go away, until you are walking this forest path with me.

If I Could

If I could I'd love to look into your eyes again
and see the love light there that once burned bright for me.
If I could, I'd like to make you smile again.
That smile that could light up every room and caused a light
to burn bright inside of me.
Here now there is only darkness and shadows are all I see.
If I could, I'd tell you of my love.
A love that haunts my heart both night and day.
A love that only you can set forever free.
If I could, I'd take back those words I said, words that made you
look away from me
And nevermore to cast your gaze on me.
If I could, I'd be the man you thought me to be and you would see the pains
that torture me.
And know that I am very truly sorry. If I Could. If I Only Could.

Seasons of Love

We have been together through so many changing Seasons, it is hard for me to decide which Season I love being with you the most. So many memories of being with you in each Season, are kept stored away in my heart. At first I think walking with you on a warm Summer day is my favorite memory. The suns rays warm me on the outside almost as much as holding your hand warms me on the inside. Your love has warmed me more than the rays of the Sun could ever hope to do. But then I remember walking with you under the Harvest Moon. Walking together under the stars on those cool October nights I told you it was the chill in the air that caused me to tremble. As a man, I was afraid to admit that just your touch could do that to me. Looking back, I believe you knew what just holding your hand or being in your arms does to me. Your playful laugh gave you away while I had to work to conceal my helplessness, whenever I am with you. Sitting in front of the fire with you in my arms made the snowy Winter bearable. Sometimes I wished the Winter would never end. So many times I blamed my teary eyes on the smoke from the fire. but you knew it was because I felt so warm, and content, and loved. Being with you in Springtime could hold the favorite place in my memories. Your unbounded happiness when you discovered the first flowers of Spring makes me smile even now as I think of it. Spring flowers are very beautiful but seeing you smile, or hearing your laugh, is the most beautiful flower of all. There is no way I can choose a fondest memory of the changing Seasons. Being with you and knowing that you care makes all the Seasons special. My heart will not allow me to favor one Season over another because it knows that I am loving you more and more with every passing Season.

Dreaming

I love to watch you as you sleep,
Your heart free from daily cares.
And do you ever dream of me,
And all the love I wish to share?
You seem so calm and unconcerned,
Your face with eyes closed smiling.
While I sit here with troubled heart,
Afraid in sleep my memories dieing.
How I long to hold your hand,
Or gently brush your hair.
To make the slightest little sound,
To let you know I'm there.
But I'll not disturb your reverie,
Nor wake you all night through.
I'll just sit here and watch you sleep,
And dream of loving you.

Quiet Times

I love those times when, as I sit on the sofa, you come and lay down beside me. I smile at how fast you can fall asleep on the pillow in my lap. I marvel at the silkiness of your hair as I run my hand across it. Yes, the years have put a silver gray strand or two in there but I would never mention it. Looking at you I still see the young girl who stole my heart away. I remember how you teased me each time we went on a date. I remember how happy I was when you told me I was the man you wanted, a happiness that has never faded through all these years. There are lines across your face as you sleep so peacefully. As I look at you I wonder if I had been a better husband, if those lines would have stayed away. Holding your hand I feel you shudder so I cover you with the afghan your hands so lovingly made. I sit here wondering what I did to deserve the love of such a beautiful woman. The home you have made for us is full of your love. I feel ashamed for not telling you more often how happy you have made me. And then from your soundest sleep, you squeeze my hand as I whisper I love you.

What is a Rose?

What is a rose? A breath of spring.
Thus heart that knows, the joy you bring.
Or is it just a rainbow chased,
Across the sky, by winds in haste?
A gentle rose, softly caressed,
Is like a man, by love possessed.
For men have hearts, that fear no pain.
They share their love, and then drown in rain.

Reaching Out Your Hand

With every passing day I knew I was drifting farther and farther away from reality. Even my old friends looked like strangers to me. We had nothing in common anymore. I was becoming a person I did not recognize and then you were standing there and you reached out your hand to me. Each night I felt cold and alone. Nothing could fill the emptiness I felt deep inside myself. There was nothing I could do to feel really warm and I did not think I would ever feel warm again. Then you were there again and you held me in your arms. While in your embrace, a calming warmth engulfed me and you filled me with a warmth that went deep down into my very soul. With each passing year, I forgot what it was to love and be loved. Only memories remained of once caring for someone, more than I cared for myself. The feelings that came with sharing the joys and sorrows together as we greeted each new day. And now you are here sharing your love with me and you have taught me to love again. My heart is bursting with love for you and all this came about because you reached out your hand to me and I willingly took it.

Before You Love

Seek not hidden meanings in my eyes,
Let your heart believe each word I say.
My love forbids my ever telling lies,
Your kisses draw me closer everyday.
Some men take love without a second thought,
They care little if they break a woman's heart.
But love is something that cannot be bought,
And man is poorer when true love departs.
I've loved and lost and then I've loved again,
Each time growing less wealthy than before.
Perhaps one day I'll learn to love again,
Her love I'll keep, no longer to be poor.
Before you fall in love beware,
Lest you cast your heart upon a thorn.
Be sure my love is true and that I care,
For can I trust this heart so often torn?

The Ways I Love You

I know how much you like to hear me tell you that I love you and I never want to forget how happy I am to tell you that. But there are so many ways I love you that you will never know about. I love you with my eyes when your back is turned to me as you work around the house. I love you with my hands as I do the chores you ask me to do for you. I love you with my mind as I think about you as I am coming home to you. Knowing you will be waiting for me, ready to share my arms around you with yours, in a loving embrace. I love you when I feel the noon day sun beaming down on my back. The warmth old Mr. Sun gives me, is like the warmth your love gives to my heart. A warmth that lasts long after the sun sets behind the mountains. I love you for being you. And if there were anything I could change, it would be me. I would give myself a voice for each way I love you and together those voices could tell you what I feel in my heart. The love that my one voice sounds so very inadequate, when it tells you," I Love You."

A Rose

To reach for you is to reach for a rose,
Whose beauty is a wonder to the eye.
But there are thorns as everybody knows,
To prick you and to cause a tearful sigh.
Still I reach for that wondrous flower,
Mindful of the pain I'll have to bear.
Love can't wait for any periled hour,
And I can stand the pain if pain be there.
But if you be elusive to my grasp,
And I must take a less than perfect flower,
Let the thorns surround me 'till I gasp,
And like a rose be dead within the hour.

A Prisoner

I am a prisoner of my heart,
With no hope of ever being free.
Loving you has been my sin,
And I'm condemned for all eternity.
You are an accomplice to my crime,
Perhaps without your knowing.
Your tender touch and calming voice,
Has started my sin growing.
And then you showed you care for me,
One of the foulest crimes of all,
For I'm a man who's easily led,
My love starved heart just had to fall.
Now I'm a prisoner without hope,
Nevermore will I be free.
My heart built walls too steep to climb,
And of loving you it's true I'm guilty.

On Aging

Each time a lady stands before a full length mirror and looks at all her perceived bodily faults, there is one thought she should keep in mind. Far away from any mirror, stands a man who refuses to look at himself in the mirror. Because men know their shortcomings from the day they are born. And men spend the rest of their life hoping a lady will look beyond all their failings and love them anyway. It is the love of a woman that blinds men from seeing the physical changes that so distress a lady. When a man looks at a lady looking at herself in the mirror and she is frowning, the man feels sadness. His sadness comes from his not being able to make that lady feel beautiful each and every day. When a man loves a woman, her portrait is hung in the warmest and brightest place in his heart and it is that portrait a man sees each time he looks at that woman. As we grow older and time seems to be unkind to us, there is that portrait and the love that put it there. A love that will never accept physical changes in a lady, as anything more than a little dust on the portrait of the woman he loves. It is up to the man to make sure the woman knows these changes do not matter. It is the love inside the woman that will always make her appear beautiful and it is this beauty that keeps the man feeling forever young.

Your Golden Years

When others turn a loving eye from thee
And you are left alone to count your days,
It's then I hope that you will call on me,
To comfort you with happiness and praise.
The years have chased your beauty deep within
Where others though they look can never see
While I know all the love that lies deep in,
The heart that never once could smile on me.
If in loneliness your heart can look again,
At a man who could not cause your heart to sigh,
Perhaps this time you'll see a loving man,
Who spent the passing years just standing by.
If by waiting I'm the last to have your love,
I'll never say that all the years were wasted
I'd pray each night to all the stars above,
And thank them for the love I've finally tasted.

Morning Coffee

Each morning as I sit across from you at the kitchen table, I like to look at the beautiful lady who has stood beside me all these years. I do not see the tired eyes and weathered features the years have placed upon your face. I still see the pretty lady who chose me to accompany her through life. There were so many men, more handsome, and more stable, than I but you saw something in me that even I didn't realize was there. You made that certain something grow until I was bursting with love for you. My eyes well up as I look across the table at you. When you ask what is wrong, I tell you it is just something in my eyes. That something is you and the warmth and love you have given me all these years. As I look at you I tell myself I should have tried harder and been more thoughtful to provide all the material things you deserved. You never complain but I know there are times you wished our lives could have been a little easier. I find my heart crying out with thanks for all that you have given me. You have a surprised look on your face as I grasp your hands and reach across the table to kiss you once more. You smile that same smile I remember seeing the first day we met. A smile that is the greatest gift you could ever give to me. My heart is smiling too as it whispers I love you.

Waiting For You

When all your hopes, and plans, and dreams,
Come crashing down as they often do.
You'll never have to face the world alone,
Because I'll be waiting here for you.
Right now you do not need my love,
You have new loves to see you through.
But when these loves all fade away,
I'll still be waiting here for you.
You have a kind and trusting heart,
While other hearts prove not as true.
But there is a heart that does not lie,
And it's waiting here for you.
Each day I pray for your happiness,
I hope all your dreams come true.
And I'll be content to see you smile,
While I sit waiting here for you.

Looking At You

Should you ever wonder if I still look at you and wonder what I see. I'd tell you of the love I feel and the love you gave to me. A love that fills this once lonely heart with a love to last through all eternity. Where you see only red, and raw, and wrinkled hands you often hide between your knees, I see a pair of loving hands, that made a home for me. Hands that cooked the meals, and washed the clothes and still had time to comfort me. Hands that turned a garden into beauty for all to see. I know you worry about the lines and creases on your face, lines that have known both smiles and tears and creases the coming years cannot erase. Each time I look at you I smile and say this silent prayer. I thank the Lord for each new day because I know you will be there. Each time you wonder if I still look at you, just look at the loving smile upon my face each time you come into my view.

Consolation

You soar through life on fragile wings,
Strong winds may make you stall.
I'm waiting here with open arms,
To catch you when you fall.
And when life's troubles seem too much,
For you to ever bear.
I'll be waiting with an open heart,
To let you know that someone cares.
Troubles don't seem quite so bad,
When a problem is shared by two,
I know because you were there for me,
As I wish now to be there for you.
Please let me help you with a kind word,
Maybe a tender hug will do.
Then you'll be ready to face the world,
With new found strength to see you through.

Forest Across The Lake

It was a picture perfect day at the lake today. Without a breeze the water was mirror calm. Houses across the lake were reflected in the water. It reminded me of the jigsaw puzzles I put together as a child. Occasionally a pair of ducks or geese would leave a trail of waves as they swam by. I could see people walking along the shore where the houses lined the beach. Off to my right across the lake, there was a stand of cedar and pine trees so dense, that they were undisturbed by the encroachment of man. It was here amid this cool forest that my mind wandered to. I knew that if I could be in that forest, I could be alone with my thoughts and memories. Thoughts of how I wish my life could have been. Memories of you and the love that we shared together. Trying to get along in life without you robs me of the quiet times I could use to be with you again. If only in memories. That virgin forest across the lake could blanket me with it's cool, dark, stillness. Hidden among those branches no one could see my tears. No one could laugh at me as I laughed, thinking of the happy times we spent together. Life goes on and we learn to accept the dawning of each new day. But there are special days, like today at the lake when I want to be alone with you. If only in my thoughts. And share a walk with you. On the other side of the lake. In the deep dark forest. That silently beckons to me.

A Lasting Love

Do not look with tender eyes on me,
Unless your heart tells you to look forever.
For I am blind with love and cannot see,
The day that you might look upon me never.
Do not let me hold you in my arms,
And shower you with tender loving kisses.
To hold you for a moment would do harm,
If my heart held you only against your wishes.
Do not calm me with your gentle voice,
If your words do not pour out from your heart.
Rather I were deaf to any noise,
That tells me we will someday be apart.
But if you look upon me any-way,
And lovingly our arms each other hold.
Believe my love will grow with passing days,
That love to keep you safe as we grow old.

Dust On The Bible

Early this morning I finally got around to dusting and re-arranging the books on the bookcases. On the bottom shelf, wedged between two books I will never read, I came across a bible. This bible was given to me when I joined the Air force, and became a Medic. Because it was such a beautiful, sunny day, I decided to take a ride up into the Pocono's of Pennsylvania. For some reason I took the bible along with me. Coming across a green field overlooking a small valley, I decided to take a walk. And I carried the bible too. Walking to the end of the field where the valley stretched out before me, I began to think and remember. There were farms doting the landscape below me. The peaceful scene caused me to remember more peaceful times in my life. Times when someone else was with me. Someone who cared for me and made me feel whole. And then too there were the memories of the sad times. A pick-up truck came roaring across the field to where I stood. In it were the farmers wife and their daughter. When they saw the bible in my hand they waved and drove off. Looking at the bible, I remembered reading it when I was assigned to work in the Air Force hospital. I worked on the terminal cancer ward. I read the bible, as a nineteen year old kid. Trying to understand why people had to die. And the bible was with me when my fiancé drowned. The years passed and the bible was on the bookcase, gathering dust, when my wife died in childbirth. We all have had tragedies in our lives. And somehow we have made it through. But standing on that hillside, with the bible in my hand, I realized there is something greater that has sustained us. Through the good times and the bad. That something is called faith. Having faith keeps us going, when we want to just give up. There is more to life than just getting by each day. The words in the bible last long after each generation comes and goes. There is faith, and hope, and love to be found in each page of the bible. Now I don't consider myself overly religious. I miss going to church for long periods of time. But for whatever time I have left in this life. I am going to keep wiping the dust off of this bible.

Your Smile

Each day you give away your smiles free,
To strangers who may pass with hollow stares.
While I would pay to have you smile on me,
And be thankful for the chance to show I care.
I do not with my payment try to cheapen,
The gift you give to others for no price.
Rather it is my heart that longs to sweeten,
The smile that it needs as it's only vice.
And I would pay to be there when you frown,
To see you when there's sadness on your face.
For I would reach and tear the heavens down,
To chase those tears and put sunlight in their place.
Willingly I'd do these things for you,
And pay my way for every step I took.
I wish only to stand before your view,
To see you smile when on me you might look.

Easter Lilies

Beside the front door, the Easter Lilies are bursting forth from the ground. The way they have each Spring since you planted them in the garden. Sitting on the front step, I can remember how you looked when you planted them. Kneeling in front of the flower bed, your face smudged with dust from the gloves you wore, your eyes aglow and your face smiling. The satisfaction you felt out of creating such a beautiful garden. The garden is still here and although I try, I can never make it look as nice as it once did. I do not have the love for flowers in my fingers that you had, but I will always keep the garden as you left it. It is just another reminder of the love you had for life and for me. Each Spring morning, as I leave the house, I smile when I look at your garden. I know that no matter how bad the day goes, your Lilies will be there to greet me when I return. And through those Lilies, I feel the love you had for me, and my heart can smile again too.

A Smile and A Tear

My heart is torn between a smile and a tear,
While love pours out for you all overflowing.
Beneath the happiness of love there lies a fear,
Will I be loved and is that love now growing?
My heart can smile with every thought of you,
For you have brought it from it's saddened past.
And it can laugh when I am close to you,
Not wondering if this love will always last.
My heart can cry when I am all alone,
For sadness comes from silent mental fearing.
To fear your love is something I may never own,
To watch that which I love slowly disappearing.
My heart is torn between a smile and a tear,
And I'm content to live this troubled way.
My heart knows only joy when you are near,
And happiness keeps all the tears away.

Coming Home

Knowing you will be home soon, I have the martinis made and chilling in the ice bucket. The dinner is in the oven, filling the rooms with mouth watering odors. You smile as you enter and I greet you with a hug and a kiss. As you head for the bedroom to slip into something more comfortable, you notice the towel covering the ottoman. When you return, I have you sit in the recliner with your feet resting on the towel. The CD player is playing the music you love so much. And I cover your eyes with a warm damp towel. You sigh as I pour the cold oil on your feet, and slowly, gently, start massaging them. By your heavy breathing I know you have fallen asleep. Letting the days problems drain from your conscious mind. I stop kneading your feet only long enough to cover you with an afghan. When I am sure you are in a restful state of peace, I go and check on the dinner I have prepared for you. Making dinner once in a while is only one of the ways I can prove my love for you. To show you how much I care. And to make you feel appreciated. In my heart I know it isn't enough. Because you have given so much of your love to me. And then the timer on the oven goes off. And I awake to find that I was only dreaming. The chair is empty. There are no odors coming from the kitchen. There is no one I can meet at the door. Someday I hope to meet a lady who would like to have someone greet them at the door. And make them feel loved and needed. And I will be standing inside that door. Ready to show her all the love I have to share.

A Valentine

This Valentine I give to all the world
so that each lonely heart will have a friend.
And though the world is large I worry not,
More love have I than I can ever spend.
If you are young and yet to fall in love,
take this love I freely offer thee.
Not as your lover who is yet to come,
but as a friend, a friend that would be me.
If you love now and love with all your heart,
I do not wish to trespass on your bliss.
Rather I would hope to mirror thee,
and show to others that which they might miss.
If you love now another who has gone,
do not think your love is unreturned.
In your smile others see there burns a flame,
whose fire once lit, will never cease to burn.
If all the world would only stop to share,
their love as I now offer to share mine.
Then all mankind would finally be at peace
and this would be a worldly Valentine.

Changes

Would you mind if I made some changes in our bedroom? I would remove all the bottles and tubes of cosmetics that cover your vanity table. Oh, I would allow you to keep a tube of lipstick. And maybe a tube of mascara. But all those other creams to hide blemishes and facial lines, would have to go. For they only hide the face of the beautiful lady I learned to love, and marry, and pass all these wonderful years together with. You were a beautiful lady then. And you are even more beautiful in my eyes now. When I look at your face, I only see love lines. The smiles and tears we shared together as we grew older have left scars on us both. But I couldn't have made it without you. And when I look at your face I still see that beautiful young girl whose love I didn't deserve to have. That picture of you stands proudly in the warmest place in my heart. And that is the picture I always see when I look at you. There are other things you can keep on your vanity table. But I won't allow you to keep things that hide the face of the woman I love. The woman whose face will stay forever beautiful in my eyes.

Because I Care

How shall I pay you for the love,
You've freely given me?
The many times you rid my heart,
Of pains that no one else could see.
Perhaps with flowers I could show,
My thanks for all you've done.
But flowers last such a little while,
And I want my thanks to live on and on.
I'd like to send you moonbeams,
Each night to dance around your bed.
To light and warm the pillows,
On which you lay your weary head.
In daylight I would warm your heart,
With sunbeams loving rays.
To let you know how much I care,
And love you every day.

Autumn Walk In The Woods

Amidst the falling leaves of Autumn, I took a walk into the Forest today. And with each falling leaf, tears fell from my eyes. These were not the tears of sadness because you are gone from me forever. Rather they were tears brought on by remembering. Remembering the many times your laugh lit up a room and made others around you smile. The sunlight cascading down through the half leafless trees shone almost as bright as those smiles you put on every ones faces. Even now I can smile through my tears as I picture you bustling around in your kitchen. Autumn was the time when your kitchen was engulfed with the odors of pumpkin and apple pies. Lovingly baked by you. The squirrels dancing around the trees reminded me of our children playing in the kitchen. Hoping to be the first to sample the hot from the oven pies. I can still see the twinkle in your eyes as you scolded them for being so impatient. You never scolded me for sneaking up on you. And with my arms around your waist, looking over your shoulders, you broke off a piece of pie crust for me to sample. Laughingly, you told me I was worse than the kids. Falling leaves covered the forest floor the way your love covered every room in the house. Halloween and Harvest decorations brought the joys of Autumn inside the house. And one could see the love you put into each and every decoration. One reason I like walking in the forest is because we used to walk there together hand in hand. And now as I walk alone, and the tears roll down my cheeks, your memory is walking along with me. And each falling leaf brings another loving memory of you to brighten this lonely heart.

Death

A candle burned,
That burns no more.
A light went out,
And closed loves door.
Loves door between,
A man and wife.
The man has gone,
Now lonely life.
But memories live,
When tears have dried.
And woman learns,
She need not cry.
The love of two,
Now shared by one.
And love she will,
'Till her life's done.
For sorrow lasts,
But a short while.
They learned to love,
She'll learn to smile.

Winter's Warmth

Outside the window the falling snow creates a blanket of white. The barren trees stand as frozen witnesses to Winter's unrelenting grip on the land. Only memories remain of warm sunny days, sitting under the shade of leaf filled trees. Inside the window there is a warmth that Old Mr. Winter cannot touch. The warmth that you lovingly provide in everything you do. There are chocolate chipped cookies, fresh baked from the oven. Steaming hot chocolate, with tiny white marshmallows floating on top. There is sitting with you on the sofa; nestled under a bright colored afghan that your hands so lovingly made. As we sit in the darkened living room looking out at the falling snow; it is so quiet we can almost hear the cold wind howling. With you in my arms I never felt so warm and contented. And I bury my face in your hair so that the silence, on this cold wintry night, will not be broken. Broken by a voice from my heart, telling you how much I love you.

Discovering Peace

Many a sight I've gazed upon,
In awe and admiration.
But nothings quite as lovely as,
The moon upon the ocean.
Sorrow, happiness and even fright,
Shared my heart on that moonlit night.
And with each glittering ocean's roll,
I felt an emptiness within my soul.
As I gazed upon the sea,
I felt that God was there with me.
And so I prayed because I knew,
That I'm among the chosen few.
Many men have searched this earth,
For peace and consolation.
But even before I'd begun to look,
God has shown me his ocean.

The Park Gate

I walked down to the lake today. But the Park Rangers would not let me in. They said I was doing something to the animals in the park. They said the birds would stop singing. The geese and ducks just sat by the edge of the lake. And the rabbits and squirrels refused to come out of their holes. They asked me what I was doing to the animals. I tried to explain it wasn't anything I was doing to them. I told them how much you loved walking along the lake, holding my hand. I told them how the ducks and the geese used to swim along beside us. Hoping you would toss bread crumbs to them. The birds in the trees would sing, as you softly sang along with them. The squirrels would show off by running around the tree trunks, making you laugh. And the rabbits would sit twitching their noses, showing off in front of you. Knowing how gentle you were, and not being afraid as we passed by. I told the Rangers I would be walking along by myself from now on. I told them that all the animals were my friends, and they missed you as much as I do. And without saying anything, the Rangers opened the gate and let me enter the park.

Hidden Tears

Each time we meet with arms entwined,
My loving heart lets out a sigh.
But I must hide my feelings with a smile,
For men are not supposed to cry.
Your kiss, your smile, your caring eyes,
Leaves me weak from love I can't deny.
You'll never see how much I care,
For men are not supposed to cry.
And when you're gone a lonely void,
Brings sadness and often tear to eye.
So I hide my face so none will see,
For men are not supposed to cry.

Daises

Today I stopped along a country lane, and picked you a bouquet of white and yellow daisies; that were growing by the roadside. I remember how your eyes would well up each time I did this for you. I smiled as I watched you place these flowers in a vase, and place them on the dining room table. When a friend would call you always mentioned the white and yellow daisies. And as the day wore on and you looked at me, I could see the love and the "thank you" in your gaze. It only took little things like this to make you happy and content. And I was happy because I remembered to do them for you. The little flowers only stayed beautiful for a few days, and I could see a note of sadness in your eyes when you had to remove them from the table. How I wished the flowers would last forever, because of the happiness they brought you. But those flowers, like relationships, only lasted for a short while. I will put this bouquet of daisies in a vase, and set in on the table. And though it too will only last a little while. The love I store in my heart for you, and the memories of your smile, will always make me smile. So long as there are Daisies to be picked, and rhythmic beatings in my heart, the memory of your love and smile, will last forever.

In Search of Riches

In search of riches I have lost, so many friendships that were tossed.
Away because I could not see, how great a gift a friend can be.
With loneliness I pay the price, of forgetting how to treat one nice.
A friend that is, didn't you know? I had so many long ago.
And now I know not how to find, the formula that once was mine.
For making people proudly say, "Welcome friend, won't you stay?"
My home is a mansion so empty and still, I can hear the rain dancing on my window sill.
Through cheating and lying I'm the richest of men, But I can't buy happiness, or one really true friend.

What is Love

Everyone has their own ideas about what love is. And there is nothing wrong with using love and sex in the same sentence. I don't know exactly what love is. To define it so that everyone can say, "Yes, I agree with you. "Having served in the Air Force, I know I love our Flag. The symbol of our Countries unity. I love what our Country stands for. There are times when it appears the beliefs of our Founding Fathers are being subverted. And used for the benefit of the few. But we will always right ourselves. Our beliefs are stronger than those who would tear us down. Love is walking in the deep Forrest. Drinking of the fresh smell of the ferns. Watching the squirrels playing tag around an Oak tree. Hearing the birds calling to each other. Love is watching a fish rise to the surface on a quiet lake. Or hearing the mournful cry of a Loon as the lake prepares itself for it's evening slumber. Love is watching your mate without them knowing you are watching them. Each little thing they do around the house that becomes routine; should receive your thank you, each and every day. Love is not taking the one you love for granted. There are three hundred and sixty five days in a year. How many times in that year do we say, "I Love YOU? "It's embarrassing when you think of it. Being single, I am far from an expert on what love is. But I think I know what love should be.

Journey's End

You wonder why I hesitate
Before letting our lips meet.
It's because I never knew that love
Could taste so very sweet.
I've drank my fill of other women
And when that thirst was done.
I'd leave without the faintest sigh
Down lonely roads to run.
Now you're a girl who's given
All the love you have to give.
To a man who's just a vagabond
Who cares not where he lives.
I should run away and leave you
Like I've done each time before.
But your love has found a way to keep
My feet inside your door.

Autumn

The coming of Autumn does not hold a sad foreboding for me. And the chill from the cold Wintry nights cannot touch my heart. I still walk with you among the falling leaves. I can close my eyes and let each falling leaf be another kiss that you give to me. A gentle breeze carries your laugh through the branches of the trees. And the warm sunlight caresses me as only you could do. The leaves may desert the trees each Autumn; but you will never fade from the branches of my heart. And Winter will not be a time of sadness, as the snows blanket the forests, where we used to walk. There is a fire burning inside me that no Winters storm can put out. A fire that was started when you came into my life. A fire that will warm me and light up the dark, stormy, Wintry nights. Your love will sustain me until with the coming of Spring; we will walk together again through a meadow of blossoming flowers.

My Heart

When I'm alone with just my thoughts,
I always think of you.
I try to hide the way I feel,
But my feelings keep coming through.
I should lock my heart up very tight,
Or send it far away.
Then I'll have some peace of mind,
And not think of you each day.
But my heart doesn't seem to care,
How much it torments me.
It only wants your loving smile,
To remember endlessly.
Now of my heart I've lost control,
It loves without my knowing.
And I must guard my every thought,
To keep that love from showing.

A Walk in the Woods

Sometimes I like to be all alone by myself. I take a walk in the woods just to prove to my heart that I don't have to think of you every spare minute. Walking along the shaded trail, the fresh smell of the ferns plays tricks on my mind; and reminds me of your sweet smelling perfume. As I sit on the stump of a fallen tree, a Blue jay dances from limb to limb above me. And then it's bleating cry, calls your name; mocking me. A tiny Chipmunk runs along the fallen tree, until it's at my side. It stands up on it's hind legs, begging for a handout. It's big, sad eyes, reminds me of you when you want me to do something I really don't want to do. I reach in my pocket and crumple up one of the cookies I carry in case I get hungry. Holding out my hand the Chipmunk comes and takes a piece of cookie. I am reminded how cautious you were with your feelings; and about trusting me with your heart. Placing the cookie crumbs on the fallen tree, I continue my walk. Entering a sunlit meadow, the warm sun causes me to shiver. The same way I shiver when I hold you in my arms,; and feel your warmth. Suddenly, a strong melancholy comes over me, and I feel very alone. The next time I want to walk alone in the woods, I hope you are there with me. Knowing that my heart will be laughing at me, is better than being in love with you; and walking through the woods without you.

I Can't Love You Any More!

I can't love you any more! And I know I'll never love you any less! Before you came into my life, I did not know what love is. You taught me how to never use the word I; and to always use the word we. And as my vocabulary grew; so too did my love for you. By giving of yourself, and caring; you took away my selfishness. And once I realized you were the most important thing in my life; I learned what true love is. I can't talk about me any more! Nothing that I do is that important; unless you are a part of it. Together we can do anything. You have instilled confidence in me to try anything in life. And to never be afraid of failure. You give me the inner strength to succeed. And I know you will be there to catch me if I fall. I can't be alone any more! You are in my heart and on my mind every minute of every day. The golden ring you placed on my finger, was not a sign of ownership. Rather it is a sign to everyone that I am loved. A sign that I am important to someone. That I have worth that strangers may not see. Because each day you show me how much you love me; I can't love you any more. My heart is filled with love to overflowing. A love that will neither fade nor grow. And you are the reason for this love.

Remembering

With arms together we would walk,
Through starless Wintry nights.
No Winter's chill would touch my heart,
Your love my warming fire light.
Men with words of hate would try,
To tear my spirit down.
But you'd be there with words of love,
And I could hold my ground.
If only I had cared for you,
As you had cared for me.
I'd have you standing by my side,
And saved you from the sea.
The days and nights pass slowly by,
I feel I'm growing old.
Your love is gone, this hollow heart,
Is cold, so very cold.

Roses

Each time I see a rose I think of you. Whenever I did something foolish, as I often did, I knew that bringing you roses would ease my guilt, and help you forgive me. One of the ways I'd celebrate your birthday was by sending you roses. And when there were times I wanted to surprise you, roses were apart of the surprise. It took so very little to make you happy; taking you out to dinner so you wouldn't have to cook or helping you around the house, but roses were the one gift that always made you smile and know how much I loved you. Even now, after all these years, I still remember your birthday by putting a rose on the pillow on your side of the bed, and in my heart I can still see you smiling.

When We Are Apart

When we are apart it's not unusual for you to wonder if I look at other women. And do I wish that you were as pretty as someone else. Yes! I do look at other women. And no matter how smartly they might be dressed; or how vibrant the personality they try to express. They all fall short of how I picture you. You have shown me what true beauty is. You have given me sight to view beauty through love. Other women are cold statues, no matter how they look or dress. Because of my love for you, and your faith and love in me; you are the most beautiful woman in the world. It really isn't fair the way I look at other women. All I see in them is their imperfections; as I compare them to you. I do not see the gentle caring, the loving concern, that you show for me. All that I am; the way I look, the way I dress, my self assurance. You have given to me. Without your love, I would be just another hollow shell of a man. Wandering around pretending to be happy. I never want to forget how my life was before you; and how happy I am now. And if I were to lose my sight today; you would still be the prettiest woman in the world to me. Because I keep a window open in my heart; just so I can look in and see how wonderful it is to have you in there.

Spring

How soft the morning breezes blow,
The naked trees whose branches show.
A bud of life, newborn there,
Foretelling Spring is in the air.
The birds from saddened songs depart,
And sing with voices from the heart.
New songs of hope sent from above,
Recalling Summers warming love.
Waking animals slowly erase,
Tired eyes, 'till there's no trace.
Of Winter's slumber to be found,
It is gone, like the snow upon the ground.
Man who has borne the Winter's might,
And suffered through each stormy night.
Like the animals is also gay,
On this the first warm Springtime day.

My Love For You

My love for you is a silent kind of love. While my heart would stand atop the highest mountain and shout your name, and tell you of my love; I must remain silent. You have given me so many reasons to love you; I'm afraid if I told them to you, you would realize I have so little to give you in return. I love you for all the little things you do. The decorations you put around the house as each holiday comes around. The way you make sure my tie matches my shirt and suit I wear when we go out. I love you for smiling when I tell you one of my silly jokes. I love you for your patience as I continually forget to hang up my coat; or leave my clothes lying around the house. I love you when we sit together and you rest your head in my arms and make me feel needed. Yes, I know a million reasons why I love you. But I remain silent and afraid. Because I can not think of one reason why you should love me.

The Sentinel

Tonight there are no stars to count,
They hide behind the clouds.
And winds that blow the leaves create,
A noise that's much too loud.
On other nights I'd walk alone,
And count those stars I'd see.
Each one would be another kiss,
That you would give to me.
Without the wind in silence deep,
Your voice I'd hear quite clear.
And always I would look around,
To see if you were near.
Someday soon we'll walk together,
Through nights that will be calm.
And I'll forget this starless night,
I spent alone in Vietnam.

Walking With You

Last night I walked with you again. The way I have so many nights before. You held my hand and told me you were not afraid of the dark; so long as I was with you. I never told you that it was you who kept me from being afraid of the dark. You said my voice and positive attitude gave you the strength to face all life's problems. But it was you who chased all my problems away. The happiness you said I brought to your life was but a tiny drop of water; compared to the ocean of happiness you brought to me. Even now, after all these years since you were taken from me; I am not afraid of the dark. Because of you I can still face life's problems. I still know what happiness is. And when I feel my inner resolve start to weaken; I just close my eyes. And you are there holding out your hand; and we walk together again. And I am not afraid of the dark.

Broken Glass

What is the music that I hear?
Where does that sound come from?
There's a gentle tinkling in my ear,
The rivers' song is being sung.
Each night by rivers waters edge
There plays a symphony
The noise made by pieces of shattered glass
Sends their loving songs to me
Mans glassy waste drifts to the shore
Then breaks upon the rocks
And with the waves and changing tides
Plays music round the clock
We can find beauty anywhere
If we only took the time to see
And should you laugh I do not care
The rivers music plays for me.

You're Feeling Sorry

There are times when we are together that I appear to be a million miles away in thought. And when you ask me what I am thinking about, I can not answer you. How can I tell you that your soft, gentle voice, blows across my mind like a warm Summer breeze. And your perfume reminds me of a field of flowering honeysuckle. And your kiss is the nectar that flows from these vines. When I am with you, time has no beginning and no end. There is only the present, and you in my arms. I can never reveal my feelings to you; when I seem to be far away in thought. I am afraid that such deep feelings may make you feel threatened and drive you away. And you may not believe you can be loved as much as I love you. A man is not supposed to be so vulnerable, as I am when I am with you. And still, I trust you with my heart and with my feelings. Another reason I remain silent; is because someday you may grow tired of being with me. I know all my shortcomings; and I would understand. But it would not be fair to you to know how deeply I love you; and how much your leaving would hurt me. I love you so much I would not want to hurt you by your feeling sorry; even as you told me goodbye.

Silently Sleeping

Silently sleeping you lay by my side, never to know of these tears that I cry.
Silently sleeping you rest on my bed, while I know your love is a lie.
You told me you loved me, and that you'd be true, you said you'd be happy
If I'd only love you.
I wanted to believe you, I placed my fears aside, I gave you my heart,
but you lied.
Silently sleeping you lay by my side, never to know of these tears that I cry.
Silently sleeping you rest on my bed, while I know your love is a lie.
I gave you two children to make our love strong,
You said you were happy and with me you belonged.
I wanted to believe you, and Lord knows I tried,
But all the whole town knew you lied.
Silently sleeping you lay by my side,
Never to know of these tears that I cry.
Silently sleeping you rest on my bed,
While I know your love is a lie.
I met your young lover, she stopped by to see,
If I was unhappy, and would I set you free.
I told her you loved me, and I loved you too,
That's when these tears started falling for you.
Silently sleeping you lay by my side,
Never to know of these tears that I cry.
Silently sleeping you rest on my bed,
While I know your love is a lie.
This anger and hurt that I'm feeling for you,
Should cause me to leave you, but what can I do?
Our two little children need us by their side,
So I wait 'till your sleeping, and that's when I cry.
Silently sleeping you lay by my side,
Never to know of these tears that I cry.
Silently sleeping you rest on my bed,
While I know your love is a lie.

Soaring

On unseen wings I soar among the clouds. Whose pure white majestic pillars, ever changing; reach higher than man should ever fly. Drifting across the land, I can only marvel at the endless fields of beautiful flowers. The forests appear to be a solid green blanket; laid down to protect all beneath, from the harshest Summer sun. Drifting along I see the ocean; clear and gently rolling. There are fish, both large and small, swimming along as though there is only the present. Free, and not caring about any impending danger that may lay ahead. Drifting along, a feeling of love blows across me like a soft Summer breeze. And you are there, the cause of that loving wind. And I am helpless as I drift along. I bask in the warmth of your love, as though it were the Sun itself. I drift along with the clouds, not knowing where, not wanting to resist the force of your love. Not caring where the wind may take me. Perhaps someday the clouds may darken, and stormy winds may send me crashing to the ground. And though I will be a sad helpless victim of the storm. I will always remember soaring among the clouds; on the wings your love had given me.

Thanking You

Each time I stumble on life's path,
You're always there to take my hand.
And the times I hurt you needlessly,
You smile and say you understand.
You've given me such happiness,
You make all my dreams come true.
And never ask me in return,
What am I going to give to you?
I have only one thing,
But it's not mine to give away.
You see I gave it to you long ago,
My heart; and it's with you everyday.

On Being Sorry

There are times in our relationship when I feel I should say, "I'm Sorry!" Not for something I did, but for all the things I didn't do. I'm sorry for not thanking you everyday for cooking the meals, and taking care of the house. For putting so much love into everything you do for me. I'm sorry I cannot buy you a big new car. Or all the clothes you admire in the store windows. I'm sorry I'm not like the men you see in the movies. I'm sorry I always seem to say the wrong thing at the wrong time. I let the chances to make you happy by saying something nice to you, selfishly slip by. I'm sorry I don't compliment you often enough when we are with our friends. I'm sorry if I take loving you, and your love for me, for granted. You are too beautiful a person to ever be taken for granted. I'm sorry I don't really listen when you talk to me. Nothing should ever be more important than listening, and understanding, when you talk to me. Your thoughts, your fears, your simple joys, should be the most important things I share with you. I'm sorry I waste these opportunities. I'm sorry if you ever think I take you for granted. You are my reason for being. All that I am, and all that I will ever be, is because you care for me. Yes, there are many reasons why I should say, "I'm Sorry!" But loving you with all my heart is not one of them. And I hope I will never hear you say, "Your Sorry!, for loving me.

This Special Rose

Far across the ocean,
In a land they call, "Down Under."
There are sights of Nature's beauty,
That leaves us all in awe and wonder.
But there is a beauty in Australia,
That all the tourists will never see.
A Rose that lives in Melbourne,
That stole my heart from me.
Through kindness, love, and caring,
This Rose brightens each new day.
And we, the poets who know her,
Know in our hearts she'll always stay.
There is a lady called, "Greeneroach,"
Who in dictionaries you'll never see.
But there's no Rose sweeter in Australia,
Than the Rose that befriended me.

Treasure Every Friend

And so the dark curtain of night falls upon another Summer's day. The songbirds are all quiet now hidden among the leaf covered branches of the trees. While I must bear alone the silence on this darkest night. Would that I could look upon the faces of past friends, to hear their laughter, to see their eyes light up whenever I entered their house. Time and passing years have robbed me of those friends. To all of you I say, "Treasure Every Friend." Guard each friendship as though it were the rising sun itself. The sun that warms the body and the heart. And when the sun descends at the close of day, that "Sun" will keep the daylight shining in your heart. And you will never know the darkness that I see, nor miss the daylight that once shown bright on me.

Before I Say Goodnight

Of all the girls I've ever met, and there have been quite a few.
I can't remember even one, who is quite as nice as you.
You never tell me how to dress, or how I should wear my hair.
You don't complain when I am late, though I know you really care.
Because you never scold me, for the silly things I do.
I find my heart is overflowing, with this love I have for you.
You are still a very young girl, and in the years that lay ahead,
We will laugh and play together, and you'll forget these words I've said.
But promise me just one thing, before I turn out the light,
You won't tell mommy what daddy said, before he said goodnight.

Believing In Love

I do not wish to trespass, on the loving memories stored forever in your heart. And I do not come with hopes that I, can offer your life a brand new start. But there are times when loneliness, can all but envelope you. And I am here with these two arms, to comfort you the whole night through. Friendship, trust, and caring, are never given easily. So I don't mind, to wait and hope, someday you'll smile on me. I too am very cautious, I have feelings people never see. But I would trust you my dear friend, because a true friend you've proven to be. Just as sunlight brightens, the dawn of each new day. Your smile brightens up my heart, and sends me on my way. We both have known the joy and peace, that being loved can bring. And I believe we were meant to love again, I believe this more than anything.

Honesty

Why does my heart keep on pretending,
And telling itself you really care?
I guess it's better to be foolish,
Than admit the truth, you won't be there.
You always said you couldn't love me,
Your honesty was plain to see.
But I refused to hear the said words,
Saying you'll never be the one for me.
At least I won't feel my heart breaking,
And see the tears shed each day through.
Someone else has my heart keeping,
And that someone else is you.

On Autumn

Autumn, the time of cooler days and falling leaves. Many people look at Autumn as the sad ending of Summer. And many people reflect on the sad events in their lives, letting the end of Summer overwhelm them. There is happiness to be found in the coming of Winter, if we only take the time to remember. To remember walking, arm in arm, with the one you loved on a cool starry evening. To hear your feet rustling through the falling leaves, and hearing your laughter echo through the clear night air. To wish upon the brightest star in the sky. The Seasons pass by endlessly, and rather than letting each new Season make us sad because of memories past, we should let those memories lift us up to be happy. We all have loved, and lived, and had sorrows. But like the brightest star in the Wintry sky, that love should shine inside us, and keep us warm and happy. Rather than looking back at Summers leaving, and be sad. We should look ahead knowing if Winter is here, Spring cannot be far behind. And like the budding of the Spring flowers, our hearts will flower anew with happiness. Fall and Winter will pull us down, only if we let it. And I know we are all stronger than that.

Blossoming Flowers

When we first met, it was like watching the sun rise on a cool Spring morning. And just as the rays of the sun chased the dew from the Spring flowers; your smile chased away all my tears. That same smile warmed a heart that never thought it would ever feel warmth again. As the sun rose higher in the sky; the flowers blossomed into a myriad of beautiful colors. And as our friendship grew, hope in the future, blossomed within me. And you became a part of all that is wonderful with the coming of Spring. Eventually the Sun tires of traversing the sky, and it falls behind the Western Mountains. But, as the darkness descends, there is no darkness in the place in my heart where thoughts of you are stored. And I eagerly await the coming of dawn, to love you, as much as I love the blossoming Spring flowers.

Missing You

Friends all gather 'round me, we party the whole night through.
They say they're glad I'm going out, and not home missing you.
They say I've never looked better, that smiling is all I do
But these empty arms keep saying, "I Miss You."
Melissa's almost five now, and Laura's just turned two.
They have their friends to play with, they seldom mention you.
I told them you're in heaven, that we can be happy without you.
But these empty arms keep saying, "I Miss You."
Time goes by so quickly, there'll be new loves to see me through.
I guess I'll learn to love someone else as much as I loved you.
I'm taking each day as it comes, what more can I do?
When these empty arms keep saying, "I Miss You."

Chances at Love

I went and sat by the shore of the lake today. Three squirrels playing in the trees behind me, stopped and asked me where I had been all Summer. I was ashamed to tell them I gave them up for a chance to find love again. A love that was as empty as the white clouds drifting overhead. The ducks and geese swam away from the shore as I approached them. What were once my friends are now cold strangers to me. Old Mr. Crow landed in the branches of the tree next to me. He started laughing at me. Apparently he knew what I had forgotten. We only have so many chances at love. And I let all my chances fly away. Well, at least the sun is still warm on my back. And the woods across the lake are still dark and mysterious. In time I will get the ducks and the geese to be my friends again. The squirrels will forgive my absence, and play around my chair again. And I will make Mr. Crow stop laughing at me. I will again find the peace here at the lake, that I have missed. And I will never go searching for love again.

Judge Tenderly of Me

Judge tenderly of me, for I am man.
Though kings look down on me, I do the best I can.
Judge tenderly of me, for I am lost.
As fool knows more than I, though many roads I've crossed.
Judge tenderly of me, for I have loved.
Though hollow now my heart, yet once I loved.
Judge tenderly of me, for I am man.
And hollow though my heart, I'll learn to love again.

To Thank You

Today I sent you flowers. And tonight you are not going to have to cook dinner. I made reservations at the restaurant you like so much. What is the occasion? What did I do now that you haven't heard about yet? Nothing has happened, all is well. I just want to show you how much I appreciate having you as my partner in life. To thank you for all that you have done for me. To thank you for making my life whole, all these years. I know it isn't nearly enough, but I hope it makes up for the times I frustrate you with my thoughtlessness. If I can bring a smile to your face, even for just this evening, it will help relieve my guilt for not telling you more often how much I love you. I have personal reasons for wanting to take you out tonight. I want others to see the beautiful lady I am married to. I want them to see the contentment in my eyes as I look at you. I want them to be jealous of the love we share. An occasional night out is not nearly enough to show my thanks for all you have given me. But the love I feel for you, the love that fills my heart to overflowing; makes me want to try. And by trying. I hope you can see the love I have for you. A love that can never be repaid by just taking you out to dinner.

On Loving You

On walks together we would take,
Beside a calm and gentle lake,
You'd ask me if I loved you.
Always I'd be slow to speak.
Your eyes would search my face to seek,
Those words I knew you longed to hear.
So many times you told me true,
How much my love would mean to you,
And I was too shy to answer back.
My shyness hid the words to say,
How my love grew from day to day,
And burst my heart with happiness.
I loved you then, I love you now,
I'd shout these words to you but how?
When death has closed your ears.

Silent Tears

When we turn out the lights and go to bed; I always wait until you are sound asleep. And then in the silent darkness, as I hold you in my arms; tears fall from my eyes. The first tear is always a tear borne of happiness. The happiness that comes from being loved by you. A love that gives meaning to my life. The second tear falls because I realize I can never give you all the things you deserve. You give so much of yourself; and ask for so little in return. I wish I could make your every dream come true. The third tear falls because I know all my faults and failings. Faults that you so patiently overlook. Failings that frustrate you and make you frown. But you never scold me. Someday I hope to become the man you truly deserve. A man who will never disappoint you. A man who will always make you happy. And on that day only one tear will fall. A tear of happiness, because I can show you as much love; as you have given me.

The Old Lighthouse

Old beacon shining ever bright,
Safeguarding seaman through the night.
Shine thy loving light on me,
And bid me safe upon the sea.
When storms and gale force winds doth blow,
Your light is always there to show,
The harbor safe as safe can be,
And from the tempest saving me.
Why can't your light shine in my heart,
To give a past love a brand new start?
And as you do with ships at sea,
Return that love safely to me.

Walking In The Rain

Have you ever walked alone in the rain? Sometimes we do it when we are feeling down. When only the storm can see our tears. And then there are times when we feel confused, and walking in the rain takes our mind off of that which is confusing us. And then, we walk in the rain with the hope that we will find the rainbow, at the end of the storm.

Life is like walking alone in the rain. Sometimes our lives are filled with blue skies. But more than once, there are storm clouds and the rains start falling. With each storm there is the hope that we will find the rainbow. And until that rainbow is found, we have the love of family and friends, to cover us with the umbrella of their love. To keep us safe during the storm. So long as we have even one friend, the storms of life cannot trouble us. And when the rains come, we will never get totally drenched. Because we have our family and friends to cover us with their love. And even if we never find that rainbow, we know the sun will be shining when the storm clouds pass by. As it always will.

The Quiet Lake

At night I wait beside the quiet lake,
Where we once walked and laughed as lovers do.
And by each star this silent prayer I make,
That I might spend my future years with you.
But you don't know the man whose standing here,
My name I've kept as secret as the night.
For my name may sound vulgar to your ear,
And my face may be a canker in your sight.
Still, I stand here waiting all alone,
Hoping to hear your footsteps on the path.
Afraid that when you see this face you've known,
You'll turn away in anger or you'll laugh.
Man is a prisoner when his heart's in love,
And he accepts the pain that he must take.
So long as he can hope in stars above,
He'll wait for you beside this quiet lake.

Rose Thorns

You do not know that I am watching you as you sit at your vanity table. I see you looking at your face in the mirror. I see you touch the lines that time and stress has put on your face. I see you frown when you touch the circles under your eyes.
So many times I wanted to rush in and hold you in my arms. To ask your forgiveness for each and every line. To apologize for the dark rings. My years of being inconsiderate, and lacking understanding; has done this to you. But with each new line, guilt has pierced my heart with Rose Thorns. And though there are more thorns than days left in our lives; I will spend my remaining days making you happy. Each time I make you smile, I will pull a Rose Thorn from my heart. You will never grow old and feel unwanted; because I will be there to tell you how beautiful you are. You will never be alone. And when you sit at your vanity, you will see me standing behind you, in your mirror. Pulling Rose Thorns from my heart.

The Sea

Damn, Damn, Damn the sea,
Damn those waves that beat upon the shore.
Man is but a drop in eternity,
The sea is so much more.
Man lives, and loves, then dies,
His ashes blown far by the wind.
The sea lives on forever,
No birth, no love, no end.
Heartless sea I curse you,
In your depths my love lies still.
And I am lonely for that heart,
That you saw fit to kill.

The Tip of Your Finger

Would you let me hold the tip of your little finger; if I asked you? By holding the tip of your little finger I would be near enough to see those lips that beckon uncontrollably to me. Those lips that promise happiness beyond my wildest dreams. To be so close to you that the gleam in your eyes would be a blinding light. And when you told me to stop; I would willingly let your finger go. Would you let me hold your hands in mine? From those hands I would feel the warmth that comes from a heart so loving that I am overwhelmed. But when you told me to stop; I would willingly let your hands go. But you must never let me hold you in my arms. Even if I asked and begged. I am a man who is careful about letting his passions go free. And if you asked me to stop; I would not hear. And no matter how hard you tried to pull away; I would never let you go.

Prince of Fools

I watch you dance with strangers, and see them hold you near,
Your arms upon their shoulders tenderly.
While I sit here in shadows, not dancing out of fear,
Still wishing your sweet arms were holding me.
Once you and I as lovers, shared a warm embrace,
And watched the sun awaken each new day.
But I the Prince of fools, let others take my place,
My blinding jealous rage, the cause you ran away.
Would that I could halt the hands of time,
And back the days to times when you loved me.
I'd spend each minute proving my love forever true,
And this repentant fool, never more would be.

Visions of You

During the day I can find ways to keep myself from thinking of you. With my eyes wide open I can see other things besides my love for you. But when at night, I close my eyes, I am helpless at hiding the love I feel for you. With my eyes closed, visions of you pour from my heart. And in each vision there is a deeper and deeper love that grows with every thought of you. My heart must think it is my friend by painting such vivid pictures of you. But in showing me your beauty, there is a tender pain. You are not here with me, for me to hold in my arms. To bear this love alone is a cruel trick my heart plays on me. Pictures of you drift across my closed eyes. Each loving picture tears at my heartstrings. But I would not open my eyes, even if I could. I see us holding hands, as we walk along the banks of a moonlit lake. I see me holding you in my arms. And I shudder with the memory of our first kiss. I knew I would be yours forever, and I hoped that you would feel the same about me. I see us on that first warm Spring day when we walked through the flowering meadow. I ran ahead of you and picked you a small bouquet of white and yellow Daisies. At first I thought I did something wrong when your eyes filled with tears. But when you put your arms around me and kissed me on the cheek; I knew everything was alright. Until that day I never really appreciated a warm Spring day. Mother Sleep has to finally take pity on me for these pictures to end. Each day, with clear open eyes, I tell you how much I love you; and how much your love means to me. But I wish that I could show you what I see with my eyes closed. To show you the pictures of love that my heart has painted of you.

Winter Wayfarer

A snowflake stopped to say hello,
And then goodbye; It's icy flow,
Fell from my chin to kiss the ground.
The wind laughingly blew by,
And caused the leafless trees to sigh,
For the Summer that is no more.
Somewhere in cabin's fires bright,
Warm their keepers through the night,
While I'm the Winter wanderer.
My body shakes, the chilling sleet,
My shoes are pressed to hide my feet,
I'm a prisoner of the Winter storm.
In some cabin far a woman cries,
For a lover lost, a lover died,
His tomb the falling snow.
When Summer comes to warm the ground,
Through melting snow at last I'm found.
She'll know that I was faithful.

Butterflies

While traveling along a tree lined lane in the Pocono Mountains of Pennsylvania; I came upon a field completely blanketed in yellow daisies. I got out of my car to walk among the flowers. A gentle breeze caused the daisies to dance to and fro. Hundreds of tiny white butterflies danced above the flowers. Occasionally landing to partake of the sweet smelling nectar. I stretched out my hand, and to my surprise, a tiny little creature landed on my finger. I held my breath as I gazed upon this beautiful wonder of Nature. I stood so silently, I felt I could hear my heart beating. The butterfly gently fanned it's wings. And I knew that at any moment it would fly away. My finger started to feel heavy from the responsibility of holding perfectly still. And then in an instant; it was gone. Being in a relationship is like holding a butterfly on your finger. You hold your breath hoping the relationship doesn't fly away. You remain silent; afraid you might say the wrong thing. And sometimes; because so many "Butterflies" have flown away; you avoid relationships completely. Still, you can appreciate the beauty of a "Butterfly" from afar. While being afraid to hold out your hand.

To Hope for Love

So many years have passed me by,
So many words left unspoken,
So many times I should have tried,
To mend this heart once broken.
But how does one erase the love,
Etched forever in one's heart?
And how not to pray to stars above,
That promised we'd never be apart?
Oh what a fool I must have been,
To think that love would last forever.
And who can tell me of my sin,
That lets me hope for love, no never.

Jealousy

When we go out together, I see you frown when I look at other ladies as they pass by. Yes, I like to look at pretty women as they go by. But you are the lady I love and respect and want to spend the rest of my life with. And you make me feel loved and needed. I like to look at a famous painting or a beautiful sunset, but I would not trade the way I feel about you for all the perceived beauty in the world. When you entered, and found a permanent place in my heart, everything I see became beautiful. Each time I look at someone else, I hear my heart saying, "Thank you for caring for me." And when other women see me looking at them, I hope they see the love in my eyes and they become jealous. Because there is someone in my heart loved more deeply than they can ever hope to be loved. And I hope they are jealous. Jealous of you.

To Dream

Each night I see you in my dreams,
And pray that I might dream forever.
To have you with me all night long,
Oh that I might wake up never!
I hear you laugh, that gentle voice,
That calms me from my daily cares.
A voice as soft as the morning breeze,
That spreads happiness everywhere.
But all too soon I must awake,
To a world without you in it
But joyful I'll greet the night,
And dream of you each sleeping minute.

Another Tear

Sometimes it is hard to be your friend. There are times when you try to hurt me with unkind words. When you lash out at everything I do or say. But I endure these hurtful moments, because I know it helps you to wash away a tear. And the times you say you don't want to see me, or stand me up when we were to meet someplace, I forgive you because I understand. And I hope it helps you to wash away another tear. The times you ignore me when we meet, when you are out with your friends. I have learned to smile and walk away, knowing you really care. You are just trying to wash away another tear. Being a friend means not taking these moments to heart, not getting angry at unkind treatment I often receive. I know you are just trying to wash away another tear. And someday, when all your tears have washed away, you will look upon your friend. And with loving eyes, you will take the time to help me wash away all my tears.

A Fallen Angel

I just found out you're back in town,
Your friends left you, high and dry.
And the happiness you went looking for,
Your fame and fortune could not buy.
You've come back home, feeling all alone,
A fallen angel that's for sure.
I've been waiting here, I'll show I care,
If you'll let me in your door.
I can love a fallen angel,
I've always loved you from the start.
I can love a fallen angel,
Won't you let me in your heart?
You've been lied to, and now you're blue,
The world's hurt you in every way.
Those city lights are dim from here,
You'll learn to smile again someday.
I'll help you find the happiness,
You left town searching for.
It's been right here, I'll show I care,
If you'll let me in your door.
I can love a fallen angel,

Of Smiles and Tears

I've always loved you from the start.
I can love a fallen angel,
Won't you let me in your heart?
You might have made a few mistakes,
But we all make them too.
You don't have to feel all alone,
Because I still care for you.
The things you've done don't bother me,
I still love you as you are.
Won't you let me in, and I'll begin,
To love you as a person, not a star.
I can love a fallen angel,
I've always loved you from the start.
I can love a fallen angel,
Won't you let me in your heart?

Christmas Without You

After all that has happened, I felt it best to celebrate Christmas at Grand mom's house. But, my 5 year old daughter pleaded with me to have Christmas at "our" house, like we always do. Reluctantly I got out all the boxes with the Christmas decorations in them. I hung the wreath on the front door, and strung the lights across the shrubbery. I then put up all the decorations around the inside of the house. As I hung the mistletoe, my daughter asked me what it was for. I explained that big guys and girls got hugs and kisses when they stood under it. My daughter put her arms around me and gave me a big hug and kiss, saying, "I'm your big girl now Daddy." As Christmas drew near, we went to the tree farm and picked out our tree. I stood it in the corner of the living room, and strung the lights around it with the white angel on top. Then my daughter helped put the tinsel and balls on the tree. Christmas Eve, I made hot chocolate and toasted marshmallows, like we always did. And with my daughter sitting next to me, we watched a Christmas story on the Television. When she fell asleep, I carried her to her bed and tucked her in. On Christmas morning, my daughter dragged me out of bed to the living room. There under the tree was the charm bracelet and the doll her mother had given her the year before. I hugged my daughter and told her I knew how much she missed her mother, and I was sorry she couldn't be with us this year. "But she is with us Daddy. She is the angel on top of our Christmas tree!"

To Be Free

In some dark and lonely canyon,
Far from sunbeams warming glow
There's a form that hides in shadows,
A sad spirit someone let go.
Do not weep for that sad traveler,
I knew it well for many years.
And I am glad to see it leave me,
For it caused me many tears.
The ghost of past, of memories saddened,
Of loves that were never meant to be.
The ghost of hate and deep depression,
Is gone, and now at last I'm free.
Once again I'm free to smile,
To walk in sunlight by the sea
To laugh today and seek tomorrows,
To hope for love with heart that's free.
In some dark and lonely canyon,
There's a ghost that once was me.
Nevermore to hide in shadows,
My heart is light, at last I'm free.

Ageless Love

I know you have quiet moments when you wonder if I still love you as much as I did when we were young. I notice how much more time you spend getting ready when we are going out. I see you frown when you constantly rub lotion on your hands. I see you hesitate when you empty your closet of clothes that no longer fit the way they used to. When I look at you today my love, I still see that smiling young lady who stole my heart away. A lady who let me date her, marry her, and love her. Even though I was the most awkward boy she knew. All that I am today is because of your love for me. I love those hands that make you frown. Those same hands that cooked the meals, cleaned the house, and still had time to reach out to me when I was filled with self doubt. When we go out for the evening I feel proud and honored that you still care for me. You always look beautiful to me, no matter what clothes you wear. Each time you feel down because of the changes the passing years are making in you. Look at my face and my lips. From these lips you will hear me tell you every day how much I love you, and still need you. Look at the gleam in my eyes as I look at you. A gleam that was put there when we first met. And it glows brighter with every passing day. The passing years can make changes to us on the outside. But the years can never change the beautiful lady I fell in love with. A lady who will stay young forever in my heart.

To One Who Is Missed

When the day has ended,
And the stars shine from above.
My thoughts are turned to only you,
And what was once a perfect love.
Yes we knew loves deepest secrets,
How to linger in one's arms
I prayed that it would last forever,
So enticing were your charms.
We spoke of only good things,
Each dream we dreamed came true.
Two lovers were never happier,
Our troubles seemed so few.
Hearts so closely joined together,
As ours appeared to be
Could never bear to be apart,
Least that's how it seemed to me.
But in the silent waters,
Of a quiet little lake
You left me alone forever,
And my heart I felt it break.
No man has known a greater pain,
Since that fatal day
When God reached out his hand to you,
And carried you away.

Before I Knew Your Name

Before I knew your name, I used to dread the coming of Winter. In the cold dark nights the glistening stars were like strangers. A million miles away. The face in the moon would look down on me and laugh; as I shivered in the cold dark night. Before I knew your name, I used to stand in the cold moonlit night, outside a farmhouse gate. Looking across the now, snow covered lawn, I could see the lights inside the windows. I could see the shadows of people moving about; through the thin veiled curtains. And I could almost feel the warmth and love that was kept from me; inside the farmhouse walls. But that was before I knew your name. Now the coming of Winter does not hold a lonely foreboding for me. The love that you have given me protects me from any Winter's chill. Now the stars are near enough for me to reach up and grasp; like friendly fireflies. That I could put in a jar and bring to you to surprise you. Old Mr. Moon has become my friend. Now I feel warm and contented, and loved; through each Wintry night. Happiness has chased all the loneliness of Winter away. Now that I know your name.

Upon Leaving

Please think of me,
While I am far away
For I will think of you often,
Each and everyday
And if at night you listen,
To the whisper of the breeze,
You will hear it say, "I love you,"
As it rustles through the trees
The sun has rays to warm a heart,
Wherever one may be
So I have but to look at it,
To have you here with me
Being with you and laughing,
Are things I'm going to miss.
But in my hearts the memory of,
Your sweet and tender kiss
I mist say goodbye and walk away,
As a mans supposed to do
But in my heart the tears are many,
As I say goodbye to you.

Christmas Gifts

Have you noticed the older we get the harder it is to buy Christmas Gifts for those we care about? Buying for the grand kids is easy. A toy, a ball, or a doll will always put a smile on a child's face. But then the task becomes much harder. Often we don't have the monetary means to buy the material things we would cherish as gifts. Monetary and Material, are the two words that started me thinking. Can you remember when we were young and the gifts were much simpler? Gifts given from the heart. But appreciated just as much as the most expensive gift we could buy. Those simpler gifts are still there for us to give. Perhaps a, "Happy Holidays" or a "Merry Christmas," spoken to a stranger we pass coming out of a Convenience store. Perhaps a little patience shown towards the person on the phone whose English we can't understand. Maybe that person feels bad because their English is so poor. Or perhaps they are worried they will be fired for not being able to communicate with us. The job they have now may be putting food on the table for the first time for their family. Our frustration and anger as we converse with them. Which is understandable. May make them frustrated and worried. It is not their fault "our jobs" were taken Overseas. We could give them the gift of patience. And instead of leaving the phone mad. We would leave feeling good because we knew we were trying to make their job easier. I could name many more ways we could show our happy feelings during this Christmas Season. And they wouldn't cost us a penny. They would be gifts, freely given, from our hearts. And isn't that what the spirit of Christmas is supposed to be?

Liking You

I like the way you greet me,
At the close of everyday
And you always cuddle near me,
In your own special way
You're just about the nicest thing,
That could happen to a guy
But I can't explain the way I feel,
No matter how I try
After each thing I do for you,
You reward me with a kiss
And I can't remember a single time,
That you have ever missed.
You always let me hold you,
You're so doggone nice to me
I wonder how I ever got along,
Without your company
I like you for a hundred reasons,
You're so nice to have around
But most of all I like you because,
You're such a darn good rabbit hound.

I Heard the Bluebird Singing

Today I took a walk in the woods. The air was cool as I walked along the shaded forest lane. Somewhere in a tree high above me I heard a bluebird singing. It was the only sound I heard throughout the forest. I wondered if that bluebird was all alone. The way so many of us are because of the passing years. And the loves we shared but are no more. If I could I would tell that bluebird not to give up hope. I would tell that bluebird that it is not meant to sing such beautiful songs without someone close to hear them. Far away in the forest there is another bluebird singing. And thinking there is no one to hear it's song. Life is full of forests where we think no one can hear our singing. But like the bluebirds we are not meant to sing alone. And if we keep faith and never give up hope, there will be someone to share our each and every song. And I thought isn't this the way life was meant to be? As I heard the bluebird singing.

A Letter of Doubt

As I sit and read this letter,
With the words I longed to hear.
I can count the times our lips have met,
As I held you near.
Even now my heart is jumping,
With the memory of your kiss
But these lines ask many questions,
That my heart cannot dismiss.
You need not worry darling,
My love for you is such;
That as I dream of you at night,
I fear I love too much.
My heart is like the brightest star,
That pierces through the night.
And being so far away from you,
It doesn't shine so bright.
Someday an unknown poet,
Will write a poem to say;
How my love for you grows stronger,
Each and every day
I am but a simple man,
Who tries hard to preserve.
The love that you have given me,
A love I don't deserve.

In Love Again

This morning I fell in love again. And you know the person I fell in love again with. Tonight I am taking her out to dinner. I'll ask for a quiet table in a corner. So I can watch her eyes sparkle in the candle light. And as I reach across the table to hold her hands in mine. I'll tell her how much I love her. I didn't know that I could fall this much in love again. But, as I was getting dressed. And I saw how neatly my clothes were arranged in my closet. I realized I had been taking this for granted all these years. Walking through the house, there was a satisfied comfort in everything I saw there. Everything I have and everything I see around me. Was put there by your loving hands. And so tonight as I am falling in love again. I hope I can make you see and feel the love I have for you. A love that gives meaning and happiness to my life. And as I stand up and walk around the table. And hold you in my arms. I hope you can feel all the love I have in my heart for you. As I tenderly kiss you. And through all the love and tenderness I shower upon you this night. I hope it makes you feel in love again too.

Philosophy for Winter

I feel a touch of winter
In that chilly little breeze,
And it won't be long before the wind
Makes scarecrows out of trees,
The animals are resting snuggly
In their lair or den,
And the birds began their journey
That leads them south again.
All that's left are the memories
Of the warmer days gone by,
When the woods were full of animals
And birds that filled the sky,
There's nothing to anticipate
As winter hurries in,
And I guess it must have been by fate
That we happen to be men,
For we must freeze and shiver
Through each wintry day,
While the dumber little animals
Sleep the time away,
I guess by being civilized
We were meant to freeze,
While the lesser animals lie snuggly
In caves and hollow trees.

It Rained Today

It Rained today. And as I walked along the lakeshore. The ducks and geese hardly noticed me. They idled their time sleeping along the shore. No one else was out walking in the rain. If anyone noticed me from inside their cabins, they would think I was a little bit crazy. But they would not know I was not walking alone. They could not guess the raindrops were washing away my tears. And those same raindrops could never wash away my memories, of how my life used to be. There once was a time when I was not alone when I walked along the lake shore. You were walking along with me. And your laugh echoed across the still waters of the lake. My thoughts drifted back to the times I would hold you in my arms, and feel your heart beating. Now I can only long for those days past. Days that are gone forever. Our memories are all we have to comfort us through the rainy days of life. Rainy days that can never wash away the love light that burns forever in our hearts. It Rained today.

On Winter

"I want to be a big old bear!"
Is what I used to say
For then I'd find a nice warm cave,
And sleep the winter months away.
I always thought that summer,
Was the nicest time of year.
For that's when natures beauty,
Decides to re-appear
In summer I would walk along,
And listen to the sounds.
Of the rabbits, birds and even bees,
As they made their daily rounds
To me the robins and the blue jay,
Would sing a symphony
And the woods were full of acrobats,
That only I could see.
I guess I wished with all my might,
For summer not to end
But as the days grew cold I knew,
I'd lost my dearest friend
There's nothing wrong with winter,
As any fool can see
But it's like the end of life itself,
To a crazy guy like me
Many things I love have gone,
Now that winters finally here.
But memories will linger on,
To keep my thoughts of summer near
Winter's very beautiful,
I grant this may be true.
Still I'd prefer to hibernate,
If it's all the same to you.

Just Because

There are ways I try to show you how much I love you. And how important you are in my life. But everything I try to do, doesn't seem like enough. You deserve so much more than I can give you. I love to meet you at the door with these two arms to hold you tight. To kiss away the tension that built up as you made it through the day. And because I love you there are no dishes in the sink. Everything is put away and the kitchen sparkles the way you like to keep it. And there are no clothes strewn among the chairs or on the floor. Everything is hung up in the closet. The way it should be. And I know how much you like having your feet rubbed, and a warm towel placed to cover your tired eyes. And I do this because I love you. I keep the TV down low as you rest your head on a pillow in my lap. And you sigh as I gently brush your hair. It is easy to do things to make you happy. Why do I do it? Because I have the love of a beautiful woman. Whose love I don't deserve.

My Falling Tears

Tears fall each time I see you sitting at your vanity table. Frowning at the face looking back at you in your mirror. A face that has made so many people happy over all these years. A face that has weathered both happy and sad times. Never showing despair or hopelessness. Always being there to keep others from losing hope. My tears fall because I don't tell you often enough how beautiful your face is to me. It is too late to kiss away all the lines on your face. But they are there because I didn't work hard enough to keep them from coming. Tears fall when I watch you put on a dress that is four sizes larger than your dresses used to be. The years may change our physical appearance. But they can never change the way my heart sees you. My eyes are blinded by the love I have for you. My tears fall because I didn't tell you often enough that size doesn't matter. It's the beautiful lady wearing the dress that keeps me feeling warm, and loved, and needed. My tears fall more frequently with every passing year. Because you never look away from the changes the years have made in me. You have not grown tired of my silly jokes. Or my forgetfulness. You still know how to make me feel special, and loved. If only I knew how to show you the love I hold in my heart for you. If only I could make you feel special each and ever day. Perhaps no tears would ever fall.

No Angel on the Christmas Tree

Outside the cabin window the snow is falling in big white flakes. There are lights on the lake. And ice skaters drift silently by. Inside the cabin we are warmed by the crackling fire in the fire place. In the far corner stands the Christmas tree. Decorated with balls and tinsel, and many twinkling lights. As I hold you in my arms on the sofa; you ask me why there is no angel on the top of the tree. I change the subject by telling you how nicely you have decorated the cabin. I thank you for taking the time to bake cookies and pies for Christmas. Again you ask me why there is no angel on the top of our Christmas tree. I change the subject by thanking you for making each holiday throughout the year so special. I tell you how lucky I am to have met someone so caring and understanding as you are. I tell you how happy you have made me each and every day. And finally, when you ask me again why there is no angel on the top of our Christmas tree. You make me tell you. There will never be another angel in this cabin. As long as I have you.

Lady on the Street

Each time I pass a lady on the street. And see the smile upon her face. I remember how you used to smile. And brighten every place. But now that smile is just a memory. To everyone else but me. It still brightens up this lonely heart. That no one else can see. And when I hear a lady's high heeled footsteps, tap tap tapping down the street. I always stop to look around, for a face that can never be. Then strangers pass without a nod. Not knowing how their passing tortures me. Once I walked along beside you. And you smiled just for me. And I told you how my love had grown, to last for all eternity. So now I walk all alone. And force myself to smile. So no one else will ever know, how much I miss your smile.

On Having Faith

Each day I thank God for all the things He has given me. My good health being at the top of the list. He does things in His own good time. I would like to walk with you and hold your hand, while you wait for God to answer all your prayers. God always does what is best for us. We just have to have the patience and understanding, knowing He is looking out for us. I would like to hold you in my arms when you have doubts that God knows what is best for you. I never ask God for anything. I always thank Him for all that He has already given me. But if I could walk with you and hold your hand. If I could hold you in my arms and hear your heart beating. I would know that God answered the prayer I was afraid to mention. A prayer I did not deserve to pray.

The Old Man Alone at Christmas

This is the Season for giving thanks for all that we have. For all our friends and family who gather around us. For strangers who pass us on the street who smile or nod at us, as their way of saying Merry Christmas to us. And then there are those people who make no outward sign that this Season is even happening. I know such a man. He is quite old, and he never seems to have any friends or family to come and visit him. I made it a point to stop and say hello to him as he was sitting alone on a park bench. After my initial friendly greeting, I asked him what he was doing for the Holidays. He stated he would be by himself, as he is every year. I asked if he was sad at being alone on Christmas. And for the first time I saw a smile come across his face. He said he was by himself, but never alone. He said he walks deep into the forest each Christmas Eve. And he kneels down. Sometimes on the snowy ground, and closes his eyes. With his eyes closed he can see into a manger, where a child was born. And he can feel the hope and happiness that this Child's birth would bring into the world. And he knew he would never be lonely as long as his faith in that Child's message was kept alive in his heart. And then the old man looked at me and said, "I may look like I am alone. But I am never lonely." As I walked away, all the Christmas lights and decorations, didn't seem as bright to me. I felt ashamed at my enjoyment of all the material gifts God has given us. And I was envious of the old man alone at Christmas.

The Green Sequined Gown

Another New Years Eve has arrived. And I watch as you get ready to go out. I smile when I see the green sequined gown, with the silver brocade, hanging from your closet door. Although it is four sizes too small for you now, you still bring it out to look at it. I see you frown as you slip on the black, straight, ankle length dress you bought for this New Years Eve. You appear agitated as you fuss with your now silver hair, and your makeup. Turning on the CD player, I walk over and take your hand. You smile as you stand up. As we start to dance, I tell you to close your eyes. I ask you to think back to our Senior prom, and how clumsy I was as a dancer. It took a few years, but after we were married, you finally got to the point where your feet felt safe on the dance floor with me. I reminded you how beautiful you were then, and how much I loved you. And I love you even more now. After all these years. All that I am is due to your having faith in me. Now as we go out this New Years Eve. Don't worry if no one notices you the way they did when you wore the green sequined gown. There will always be one person who can't take his eyes off you. Someone who loves you very much. And as we embrace and kiss in the New Year; I will be the luckiest man in the room. Because I have the love of such a beautiful lady.

This Band of Gold

This band of gold promised we would be as one, forever. And I proudly wore it as a sign of our love; and our happiness. And when we were apart, I only had to look at it, to have you here with me in my thoughts. And when strangers asked me why I was always smiling. I would hold up my hand and show them this band of gold. This band of gold meant that I would never be alone. And if life's problems started to bring me down; you would always be there to pick me back up. You gave me a reason to try and never be afraid of failing. This band of gold meant that you would always have someone who loves you. Someone who would tell you how beautiful you are. Someone who would always listen, and try to understand your feelings. A friend who would never laugh at you; or belittle you. Someone who would tell you every day how much he loved you. And how happy you have made him. If this band of gold were made of paper; it would not matter. I would still wear it proudly as a sign of my love for you. Paper would not last very long. While gold is made to last forever. But even if the gold wore away, and the ring fell off my finger; my love for you would still remain. But what of the band of gold I put on your finger? Was it too small? And did it hurt your finger? Did your promises of love make the ring too heavy? So that you had to take it off. In time, I too will be able to take off this band of gold you gave me. But I will never be able to take off this band of love. That I will wear forever around my heart.

This Heart Full of Love

Sometimes I want to shout your name. To tell you of my burning love for you. And then with a loving voice I whisper low. That voice to tell you of my heart's refrain. It is from this heart all loving thoughts of you are stored. And treasured as I treasure all your smiles. I am a Pauper when I am all alone. Lost in a darkness that hides your face from me. Sometimes the cold and darkness is more than I can bear. Longing for the warmth and sunlight that only shines when you are here. Would that we could always be together. So that I might never feel this cold. Never feel so all alone. And wrapped in my arms you would never feel the Winter's chill. Nor know the sadness that loneliness can bring. While holding you close you can see the love light burning in my eyes. And hear loves sweet rhythm coming from my heart. A heart waiting full of love. Saving all it's love for only you.

To Ask Forgiveness

Today I told you that I'm sorry. For all the things I should have done. For all the times I hurt your feelings. And laughed as I watched those tears begun. But now I see that I was foolish. That all your tears were killing me. And now I'm sad and broken hearted. The biggest fool for all to see. There is love I never showed you. A love I've hidden jealously. If it's not too late I'd like to see you. To ask you please, to please forgive me.

Walk with Me

Come walk with me and hold my hand. And I'll protect you from the troubling storms of life. When we were young, our family was there to protect us with the umbrella of their love. And the gathering storms could never reach us. Could never drown us with trials we couldn't see. When at last we left the protection of family. And embarked upon the road to make a family for ourselves. We had the love of our partner. And together we weathered every storm. We traveled through life enjoying many sunny days. And when the storm clouds gathered we had the strength to avoid those rainy days that might have dragged us down. But now the years have past. And many times we feel helpless. We feel alone as each new storm approaches. And just when you feel there is no one there to help you. I hope there is someone like me. Willing to cover you in his coat of love. And you will feel warm and contented. While the storms around you rumble past. And I will still be there when the sun finally breaks through the clouds. And you can feel your heart is trouble free. As you take my hand and walk with me.

What I See

There are times when I am home alone. You are away shopping or getting your nails or hair done. But, you are still here with me in my mind. And in everything I see. There is the small pillow on the sofa. The one you use when you lie down with your head on the pillow in my lap. I love gently stroking your hair as your heavy breathing shows me you are fast asleep. In the kitchen there are the potholders hanging next to the stove. Those same potholders that are a part of you as you make so many delicious meals. I have to be careful when I'm in the bathroom. Careful not to tip over the myriad of bottles resting on the shelf above the sink. Perfumes and lotions that you use to keep yourself looking so nice. I wonder if you know that I would still love you if the shelf were empty. Next to the bed there are your fluffy slippers. They look like they should keep your feet warm. But when you slip out of them and come to bed. You always have to warm your feet by holding them against me. I wonder how someone so warm and so caring; could have such cold feet. Although you may be away from the house. You are always here with me. And you will always be here with me. Because of the love I hold for you in my heart.

4th Of July

For something to do I drove down to the Delaware River, on the Jersey side. Looking across the river the Philadelphia Skyline was impressive. And then the 4th of July fireworks display started. The bursting rockets lit up the sky, the way you lit up a room when you entered. The noise of the exploding rockets reminded me of your laugh. An infectious laugh that made others smile. There is an anxious pause between each ascending rocket, anticipation for the next display, after coming home from shopping. Thankful that you returned home safely to me. And then the fireworks display was over, and I started to drive home. But I did not drive home alone. I had loving memories of you to keep me company.

These Arms

There are many ways to let you know how much I love you. But the way that I can show you love the best; is with these arms. With these arms I would hold you close when the thunder and lightning dances about. With these arms I would protect you from the storms fury. With these arms I would comfort you when a movie makes you sad; or when you feel melancholy for reasons a man could never understand. With these arms I would raise you up and steady you on a pedestal; when life's doubt and uncertainty would make you want to fall. With these arms I could feel your heart beating when you are excited; and shaking with joy. With these arms I would know true happiness; because you let me hold you. And when you are away there is a sadness and longing in my heart; because these arms are empty. Arms that have a purpose and give my life a meaning; only when you are in them.

Forever Springtime

How strange it is to feel the warm sun beating down on my coat-less back. The cold days and nights of winter are finally over. Spring, the time of renewal, is finally here. The birds are back from their southern journey; and fill the air with their joyful songs. Flowers awake from their winter sleep; and break through the ground that was their blanket. They cover the ground with their long anticipated variety of colors. Spring is truly the time of rebirth and renewal. And you, my love, show your happiness at Springs' arrival in many different ways. But you always question my quiet reserve that I show with the coming of Spring. It is because it is always Spring, in the place in my heart where I keep you safe from the changing seasons. In my heart you are never troubled by summers heat that robs your face of it's youthful beauty. Your smile does not fade like the flowers in Autumn. Your laugh remains while the birds fly south. And all through the cold, harsh winter; you maintain your ever blossoming beauty. The way the few brave flowers do; as they stand tall amidst the falling snow. In my heart it will always be spring for you. So long as I can endure the changing seasons, and my heart keeps on beating; you will know the joys of spring. Everyday is spring for me too, my love; so long as I can look into my heart, and see you safely there.

A Cloud

I saw a white, billowing cloud, pass overhead today. It was all alone in the clear blue sky. How strange it seemed for something so beautiful to be up so very high, and all alone. While looking up, I wondered if you were all alone too. Could you look down and see that same cloud that brought back so many warm memories of you, to me? Every day I think of you. And like the cloud, it is something beautiful that causes these memories to come to life. Yesterday it was walking through the flowering meadows, where we used to walk. A timid rabbit, with it's nose twitching, cautiously watched as I passed by. And then it hurriedly ran away. I was reminded how timid you were about trusting me with your feelings. And how happy I was when you finally trusted me with your heart. And then I became the timid one. Afraid that I would do something to, like the cautious rabbit, scare you away. Every day it is something different that starts the memories flowing into my conscious view. Someone's laugh may cause me to look around, hoping you are there. The sunlight warming my shoulders, the way your arms warmed me when we embraced. Standing in front of the greeting cards, reading those words of love; looking for just the right one that I would have given to you. Of all the ways I am reminded of you; that tiny white cloud is my favorite. Because I had to look up to see it. And by looking up, I am looking up to where you are, hopefully looking down on me.

Another Autumn

Autumn is here again in all it's natural beauty. The changing leaves on the trees paint colorful pictures that we can enjoy for free. No art museum could hold all the colorful paintings mother nature provides to us free of charge. Walking along the lake, the ducks and geese seem to know there is a change in the air. They are more friendly to us humans, as they follow along hoping for a piece of bread. More stately beggars we will never see. The cool evenings have changed the waters in the lake to a bright clear blue. It is easy to spot the varied species of fish as they swim along. Soon they will have to find the deep pools that will keep them safe through the freezing winter. Songbirds that are usually so numerous around the lake, have already left for their southern retreats. And they are replaced by an utter silence. A silence, that gives us time to think and reflect on warmer days, and happier times. Old man winter is definitely just around the corner. And we must guard against letting him get us down. Besides our friends, we have our memories to keep us strong, and provide solace through each wintry day. The coming of winter can chill us on the outside; but it can never extinguish the fires of loves, and lovers lost, that will always burn deep within our hearts. Fires that will warm us and keep us safe; until the spring flowers burst forth and make us smile again.

If You Could Love Me

If you could love me, you would find a loving man walking a step behind you. But staying close enough to whisper in your ear. To tell you how beautiful you are. Not the beauty that fades from your face with every passing year. But the inner beauty that only your family and friends can see. A beauty that can never fade away. If you could love me, you would never stand alone in the darkness. Fearing the shadows that fill you with self doubt. For I would be there holding a candle, to light the way, and to reassure you there was no reason to have doubts. I would chase all those shadows away. And you would always walk in sunlight. If you could love me, there would always be a strong pair of arms to hold you steady as the winds of life tried to knock you down. I would protect you from all life's storms. And give you the strength to face each and every storm cloud that came your way. I would make you feel safe. If you could love me, I would help you greet each new day with a morning kiss. And you would be told how much I love you. And how happy you have made me. And yes. A steaming hot cup of coffee would be waiting for you on your nightstand. As another way to show you how much I love you. If you could love me, I would spend each new day making you happy. And never letting you feel the pain that being alone can bring. You would feel appreciated and loved. And you would know that there is a meaning to your life. A life meant to be filled with happiness. And what would I ask for myself? Nothing. All my hopes and dreams would be fulfilled. If you could only love me.

Of Smiles and Tears . . .

There is a land within my mind,
where you are free to roam.
Judge me not by what you've seen
for what do you call home?
Judge me only as a man,
who's lived with human fears
Please be kind for you've just seen,
my land of smiles and tears . . .

Edwards Brothers, Inc.
Thorofare, NJ USA
October 5, 2011